To The Wren Nesting

To The Wren Nesting
and other poems

Kristine Hartvigsen

Muddy Ford Press
Chapin, South Carolina

TO THE WREN NESTING. Copyright © 2012 by Kristine Hartvigsen. All rights reserved. Printed in the United States of America. No part of this book may be used or reproduced in any manner whatsoever without written permission except in the case of brief quotations embodied in critical articles and reviews. For information, address Muddy Ford Press, 1009 Muddy Ford Road, Chapin, South Carolina 29036.

FIRST EDITION.

Library of Congress Control Number: 2012940508

ISBN: 978-0-9838544-1-8

Acknowledgments

It is with immense gratitude that I acknowledge the friends and family who have provided me with their love, support, and encouragement, including: Gina Langston Brewer, who is the creative inspiration for several of these poems; Cindi Boiter and Bob Jolley, who never let me stop believing in myself; Jodie Gochnauer, who has embodied true unconditional friendship since we met overseas so long ago as military brats; my late mother, Carolyn Mills Rice Hartvigsen, whose love and confidence in my ability never wavered even when my attitude and actions proved less than deserving; my aunt, Gail Rice Deal, who has carried mom's torch, providing comfort and guidance beyond measure; and my sister, Heidi Hartvigsen Carr, whose strength and grace in surviving cancer give me renewed hope. I'd also like to thank poets Kwame Dawes and Ed Madden, whose thoughtful input during the University of South Carolina's First Book Project back in 2004 helped me see more clearly how I could breathe new life into my work and reach greater heights of expression.

Dedication

With boundless love and affection, I dedicate this chapbook to my son, Colin Erik Anderson, who inspires me every day with his devilish wit and big bear hugs.

Contents

untitled	1
bahnhof	2
just like	4
shower	5
Soul Mate No. 572	6
tebe	7
Waiting in Front of a Diner	8
The Stone	10
haiku 1	12
drummer at the red tub	13
Eatonton, Georgia	14
horizontal hold	15
Long Island City	17
noreaster	18
chemistry lesson	19
Art Bar Ramblings I	20
giving myself over	22
Climbing the Sides of a Mixing Bowl	23
Apparition	25
nocturne for the ether	27
Reflections on Eating a Maraschino Cherry	28
Piñero	30
ruby	31
to the wren nesting	32
security check	33
Soul Mate No. 222	34

slow descent	35
haiku 2	36
unsaid	37
walking my shadow	39
surrogate	40
sleep bar	42
equestrian	43
nebula	44
4:30 a.m., interstate 26 heading west	45
Soul Mate No. 760	46
peeling	47
Anastasia	48
Art Bar Ramblings II	49
Myrellen's Coat	50
failure	52
lotus revisited	53
peppermint	55
haiku 3	56
sparrow	57
nesting instincts	58

Introduction

To the Wren Nesting meanders through two decades of creative experimentation by a self-taught poet who came late to the dance but continues to learn new steps in her post-midlife years. Subjects here have been harvested with life's widest butterfly net from across the spectrum – anything that moved the writer's spirit to expression. These poems tell stories launched in random moments such as passing a sexy stranger on the sidewalk, having a spontaneous wave of grief after viewing a news clip, buying a book from a vendor on a Manhattan street corner, dreaming about a Frank Lloyd Wright dog house and a 19 percent raise while on pain medication, or – yes – discovering that a pair of Carolina wrens have set up house on your front door wreath. They run the gamut from dark and brooding to meanderingly reflective, heartfelt to humorous and even teasing as they depict stories grounded in moments from everyday life.

To The Wren Nesting

untitled

the girl is near plain
like her mother's kitchen table
with the fat formica top
and ribbed steel sides

except she has freckles
like the chipped blue laminate

wan but not totally

indecipherable

bahnhof

to gina and kevin

two faces in frame
foreheads cocked, touching
she leans into him
shoulder raised, she is
coy, giddy, playful

on to the next spire
across the countryside
loving, laughing, learning
sipping hot kaffee
feeding each other strudel

fused at right angles
pulp wood bonds
a child's happy watercolor
blushing innocence fresh
as a stand of cottage sunflowers

red wine and a four-poster bed
facing east, air currents
carry the scent of patchouli
and sandalwood from her hair
lightness in bright red sandals

this is bliss
the embrace of time
slow movement of soil
fresh petals leading
to the next summit

and there is music

always

just like

in the movies
the breeze lifts my hair
in a flattering way
and he extends his elbow
inviting me to link arms
as we walk along the river

the bliss of this moment
is echoed in the swaying tendrils
of street willow and birch and the
gaze of polite strangers passing by
who understand that we must be lovers

shower

morning stillness
quiet as snow
bedclothes under winter coat
I recline beneath
a wash of stars
gazing up at the trails
left by Leo's dust.

Soul Mate No. 572

long sideburns
sunglasses like Bono
his self-assured swagger
hushes the room

or is it just me

shaken not stirred
bottomless eyes
how do you spell gristle
portrait or landscape
I have to know

he's definitely a runner-up
I'll call him

Soul Mate No. 572

tebe

appalachian poet carries
his insides around in a plastic
polka-dotted bread bag
an elegy whispered
through lips moistened by fiddlesong
he scribbles on napkins, receipts,
any medium can become a gum wrapper haiku
tall hunching wordsmith
the smell of woodsmoke in his hair
shuffles feet, shuffles papers
reads without accompaniment
simple flapjacks on the griddle
plucks what he can to season the iron

Waiting in Front of a Diner, Manhattan November 1995

With swollen feet, I shift my weight and scan the sidewalk for signs of him coming from the north, on lunch furlough from the midtown skyscraper where he punches a clock. Proud of my swollen belly, now, I am draped in the matronly attire that they sell to women like me in department stores around town.

He is late, and I am hungry for some rare red meat. A street vendor peddles wares at a table by the curb, and I give two dollars for my unborn son's first book. Across the way, people sit on benches in the sun eating lunch out of paper bags and watching the cabs run in place at the gridlocked intersection. Earnestly I skim the rolling waves of foot traffic along both sides of the street.

The baby wedges his foot into the top of my ribs, and I push down hard with my hand below the diaphragm, trying to force a retreat. Finally, I spot my husband walking briskly in my direction, skirting the tourists and office workers. He looks ill at ease in his white collar uniform. When we met, he owned only two pairs of jeans – torn – a guitar, and a hundred or so record albums.

My heart quickens with pride at the sight of him, sporting a cursed tie for the welfare of our family. He looks tired, flushed from the 11-block trek. As our eyes meet, he grins and puts a protective arm to my back as we move across the sidewalk into the diner. He rambles about a last-minute task at the office and the cow-like tourists as we slide into a booth. He takes my hand across the table, and I feel certain I've never loved another human being so perfectly outside of this moment.

He scolds me for ordering a soda and suggests greens for the baby. Sharing a slice of key lime pie, we make plans to purchase a bassinet after work. We decide to meet on the subway platform at 59th and Lex. At the corner where we must part, a bus spews diesel fumes, and he leans into me. We are just another couple kissing goodbye on a New York street. No one takes much notice. I watch the swell of people close in around him on the sidewalk until he disappears altogether. I turn and navigate my way down 42nd to my tiny, windowless office in the Daily News building.

I pass the giant globe in the center of the lobby and think of Atlas. As I wait for the elevator, I feel the vibration of trains moving through the layered catacombs beneath the city. I like the orderliness of it – the rhythm, the scheduled stops, the warning announcement that the sliding doors will close. Our baby moves again. He is restless. And I feel uneasy, combined with an inexplicable weariness. In sensing the rumble of steel and cement far below, I can't possibly foresee the wreck that awaits – how my gentle husband, inside a year's time, will subtly prod us onto the tracks, me and my baby, facing down a train.

The Stone

> *Everyman has a name,*
> *and it is Isaiah.*

> *Paper, scissors, rock.*
> *The stone tells his story.*

A lone crow glides across the empty schoolyard,
its feathers a shiny mass of black ink.

Denial, bargaining, acceptance.
Where is the anger?

The crow atop a jungle gym,
stares into the snowgray distance.

Everyman knows complacency;
it sleepwalks through the hailstorm.

> *Paper, scissors, rock.*

The sullen mantra of red
prevails on this dark day.

A mother cannot find her legs
and is helped into the sanctuary.

Is Everyman listening to this
open-casket public address system?

Ashen faces seek solace
in teddy bears and flowered crosses.

A lone crow glides across the empty schoolyard.
Something long dangles from its beak,

an olive branch.

> *Everyman has a name,*
> *and it is Isaiah.*

> *Paper, scissors, rock.*

haiku 1

the dingo presides
over academic life
will I get tenure?

drummer at the red tub

softness and sinew
white teeth, brown skin

he drums with authority

footfalls on a dusty path
only a lion hears
the skipped beats

this is the gospel of sound
tectonics of the diaspora

since the beginning
it has been so

Eatonton, Georgia, July 1996

Anesthetize the babies
so they will be protected.

Give them morphine tea
so they may be prepared.

> *There will be no fishing in the lake
> of the everlasting fire.*

The church sign is near choking
under tentacles of kudzu.

Sleep soundly, child.
Do not make any noise.

Seek tranquility on this steamy afternoon
somewhere between Macon and Augusta.

horizontal hold

narcotics kill the pain

my mind a barren pool
rusty ladder descends
into earth and weeds

three lesbians gather lumber

together they build a
frank lloyd wright doghouse

monogamy – monotony
one is cheating on her husband

I dream of
my dead father
a fire engine
leonard nimoy
and a 19 percent raise

my carpet is the
state fair for roaches

city pigeons die quietly
on my windowsill
heads tucked neatly into wings

loose audio tape
lies in a tangled
pile at my feet

am openly seduced
by a nude body without a face

head pounding
clock ticking
blood pumping

bring me down
where I can feel again

slide a tennis ball onto
my flailing antenna
and help calm all this static

Long Island City, January 1996

Outside I hear every flake of snow hit the ground.
I can smell the glue on every envelope,
hear the flapping of tiny insect wings,
feel the murmur of earth breathing in sleep,
and taste elements of nickel in the humidified air.

The baby rolls beneath my tight, itching skin,
lodging his foot in my ribcage, as always.

His father sleeps beside me,
oblivious to all this racket.

I glance at the clock and sigh.
Four more hours until light breaks
on another day of weary waiting.

I doze and dream of lime sherbet
until damp sheets and understanding mingle.

I switch on the bedside lamp, turn to
my squinting husband and say,

I think it's time.

noreaster

I am the monarch of exasperated sighs
a japanese maple trapped in the body
of a great and gnarled oak

the abundant soft flesh of my trunk pours over
my old-woman shoes like loose bread dough
and my lungs fill with the unwashed stench of cities
a pungent mixture of urine, sour milk, and asphalt

my wide arbor scrubs clean what the locusts carry

pigeons dart and swoop below my branches
their erect tails portending another noreaster
even the buildings have turned up their glass-and-steel
    collars
against the bitter cold and whatever the ocean may bring

like me, this liver-spotted city has weathered much

hard rain, like the blood of estrus
pounds conformity like a migraine
but I can carry this weight and more
I stand firm against the elements because

I am not about to breathe my last

chemistry lesson

call me brazen

I would leave our bed
moist linens echoing sighs
your skin begging my return

I pause to taste you once more
in a kiss of leavetaking
and do not bathe
but run a brush through my hair
and throw on a loose shirt

head propped sidelong on the pillow
you comment on my moxie,
that I would go out now, audaciously,
still doused in our carnal mist

but I am late for a gathering of writers
and it would be a pity so soon
to erase this happy evidence of you

I shall sit among my perfumed colleagues
musky and damp with your recent presence
and I shall exude satisfaction

I will revel in the knowledge
that your sweet molecules
are all over me still

dancing on my skin

Art Bar Ramblings I

Nirvana and shadow cross the threshold to mesh wicked and sweet. Engrossed in their own secular dramas, no one pays particular attention. Absently I peel away the label on my Budweiser and gaze into this glowing GI Joe lunchbox. I don't need fluorescent hologram glasses to see why I crave this place, my arrested-in-chains, techno-rave addiction. Buzzing Led Zeppelin colloquy – mindless, intellectual exchange of wit and political correctness – commences in quad. Andy sits, head bent, scrawling tiny letters across a lined legal pad. A suggestion of beard eclipses my intuition about him; I long to read the script.

Remnants of lost sexual revolution float across the wall like self-perpetuating amoebas. No sex without scuba suits, and the art of plenary language gains an enlightened new handhold on our species. Jose soars in blue-black illumination, hair defiant as it rolls and ebbs, hiding part of his primal, feline animal-ness. I am attracted to something in everybody here. A pretty, waifish girl moves gracefully, hands airborne, expressive, in a solo reggae mind-trip across the black room, where everyone gets in touch with their psychodelia.

I know the bartenders by name – and most of the regulars. Think I may invest in leather. I watch Brett, in his ever-present Mardi Gras beads, spill coffee across the brushed metal counter. He madly clutches his head, trying to filter drink orders channel-surfing through the euphonious snow. Art Bar theme song: "We're never gonna survive unless we go a little crazy." And I listen, squinting so as to hear better, while Gregory discusses German philosophers. He reveres Nietzsche, and we agree the man was widely misunderstood. Buzzed and reflective, we clink bottle-necks in homage to the great thinker and his meandering thoughts on religious neuroses and gender ambiguity. "What is done out of love always takes place beyond good and evil." From the wall, Danielle Howle and Hick'ry Hawkins flirt with the abstract allure of celebrity

Saturated from psycho-intellectual banter, I shuffle into the cave-like dance room and begin to bounce from gentle rhythms to frenzied, head-banging, glorious abandon. Into the dark morning, nicotine settles in my clothes and hair like fine volcanic ash. I drink ice water and try to tame the ringing in my ears. I feel safe, looked after, as Ed utters that familiar parting admonishment to drive safe. I savor this place because it, and the people, however distinct, never boring, are real.

But still I have to pinch myself.

giving myself over

blinds drawn
I give myself over
to raw despondence

rolled newspapers litter the yard
and I care nothing for the hungry kitten
or the rain gutter in need of clearing

soothing voices tell me to lie down
trust the comforts of this quiet enclave
let the soft linen currents take me

Climbing the Sides of a Mixing Bowl

Flour makes a home
in the dried crevasses
of her uncomplaining hands.

She pounds, kneads,
Pauses to sift.

The mound of dough
is dry and unyielding.

Undaunted, she plunges
her fists again and again
into the hardened mass.

From all directions,
shiny kitchen appliances,
like funhouse mirrors,
reflect back her likeness.

Thin. Fat. Short. Tall. Crying.

Disfigured.

Here stands a
barren
woman.

No child will suckle the
absent
breast.

Only after months can she really look

And still she cannot bear
to touch the dark and purple
of her own tender flesh.

Fine, petal-soft powder clings
to the stainless bowl.

In purity and stealth,
it upends her by surprise
and sends her careening down
the steely slope once more.

Apparition

As a theater, the city looms blue,
reflective against the somber features
of a distant spirit strolling.

Eyes lowered, he drifts into view,
hands passively joined at the back,
his gait slow and uncomplicated.

He wears heavy clothing always –
July heat or January cold –
draped across weighted shoulders.

His austere features pluck from my darkest imaginings
icons from the horrors of long-ago conflicts.

> A naked girl running down a dirt road.
> The kneeling man, wincing in the face of execution.
> The defiant skeleton of a bombed-out church.

Blistered feet respond to the vagrant's mantra –
keep moving, keep moving.

He must be sore, weary, hungry.
But his face conveys only
a staid and somber calm.

When the light changes from red to green,
I ease across the intersection,
his hooded face framed in my rear view.

And my mind shifts
to the scattered gale
of an olive-colored helicopter,
lifting an anguished people
off a crowded rooftop
toward freedom.

nocturne for the ether

in the mountains, she shows me the ocean
our faces tingling from too much sun, we wade barefoot
into a rolling sea of poppies that reach to our shoulders
a brilliant wash of pink and orange swells
soothing us with soft petals and wind sounds

like the tides, she surrenders herself to moments
and the raw pull of lunar energy
we extend our arms wide to fan the
swaying blossoms with our outstretched fingers
gliding along in a willowy breast stroke

her gift is the life force of rain
there is no pretense in loving purely
her swift moon current carries us both
ginger tendrils lift in the moving ether
float loose about her glowing skin

what the sea takes, the sea will give again
sunlight will burn through the clouds;
beachcombers will return
looking for shark's teeth, seashells, and divining rods
ocean waves once crashed upon this high-up place
where we now wonder at a shoreline teeming with flowers

reflections on eating a maraschino cherry

it is rich and intoxicating,
this evening and me
feeling my power
long slitted black dress
flash of stillettoed calf

I like that he touches my hair
strokes it softly
the suggestion of
long fingers from behind
and I can feel him already
yet we haven't even kissed

in my drink a
cherry floats among
the ice cubes

I grasp the stem and
appraise the glistening fruit
poised above my mouth
sweet promise of moisture

my tongue fingers it
for a moment's
consideration
of carnal possibility
before my mouth

lips softly parted
takes in the orb
and rolls it
around
slowly
until
I must
break
the
skin

Piñero

the living of it seared
like a drop of Chinese water
popping on a white-hot skillet

and the steam felt
even the pain of that

nicotine fingers snuff out
gilded thoughts, caramelized visions
and the well-meaning muse
whose mistress waits at the dock
in steel-blue stiletto indignation

he sees the brass ring
through long strings of hair
steel bars and memories of *madre*
the cloak of back streets
and lengthening alleyways

proud, fallen scribe
even in death
he is dismissive

ruby

conceived in
folksong
she was a
sweet-faced
tow-headed
barefooted
little nymph
who loved
to run bare
through fields
of clover
and weave
a fairy hat
of purple
wildflowers
they called her
ruby river
her currents
ran swift
and channels
cut deep
through
the canyons
of her guitar

to the wren nesting

in my front door wreath
your visit is timely as I
have been grasping
for something optimistic

why you would choose this
motorway going through
your country garden
is a mystery to me

four powder blue eggs
in a bassinet of kindling
very soon there will be
hungry mouths to feed

you tolerate so well
our comings and goings
despite the bulldozers
and the hard hats

we are the ones
who continue to build
beyond the fragile dunes
and deny what the oceans tell us

still, knowing you are there
makes me ... happy
my sweet feathered squatter
tending your twigs and bits of down

are you subletting from me
or is it the other way around?

security check

unshowered and smelling of patchouli
she holds open her woven hobo bag
lackadaisical before the inspector

there are things this girl
doesn't leave home without

like smokes, sharpie pens, and condoms
loose change, bic lighter, sketchpad

and the useless key
to a hotel liquor cabinet
from that trip to Belize

there's a ticket stub and the cork
from a bottle of pinot noir
drunk from paper cups
on a paramour's sailboat
before skinny dipping
under a playful moon

toothbrush, harmonica,
two broken crayons, arcade tokens

and when they ask for identification,

she reaches up,
plucks a long, curly red hair,

and hands it over

Soul Mate No. 222

since when has crass been sexy?

stubble-faced guitar bravado
cowboy-booted stud seeks mother figure

he is skinny and wrung tight with
an erection his sole topographic offering

eye contact equals foreplay
and we decide to play through

no argyle pretense
we carry our own clubs

safe from the sand traps
and the trappings of obligation

love that wide grin as he
holds a pick in his mouth

tips his hat at me

yup, he's made the list
my Soul Mate No. 222

slow descent

she peered out the window
with tired eyes into the busy night
of search lights and shifting landscapes

the ground radiated upward
like dying coals on a campfire
their embers flickering in the
wake of jet-washed evening

haiku 2

I am so damned tired
how many times must I whore
myself out for art?

unsaid

I saw him today,
and it made my stomach quicken

it's been years
and still I wonder
at the easiness of his gait
the way his slender fingers
stroke the belly of a long-haired dog
and how his thick, dark brows
furrow just so when he reads.

he was sitting in one of those breakfast places
with his nose in the editorials
chewing on the end of a number two pencil

covertly I scanned
the line of his jaw
with its sunday bristle
the fine contours of his face

watching him read and sip coffee
I longed to stroll over
and start an easy conversation
but easy never was a part of us

I wanted to tell him I'm ok
because I know that

like me

he still wonders

but instead

as before

I just slipped away

misty

and

unseen

Walking My Shadow

With a stiff ladder-back chair my only comfort, I walk to ease the ringing in my ears. Drought has given midsummer lawns the look of winter. I am in the mood for a little hausmusik. The swallows will return any day now. I am almost certain of it. And I soon will feel refreshed, wear gingham, go barefoot, drink creek water, and make angels in the tall meadow grass. But until then, I'll be out walking my shadow.

surrogate

light a candle
pour some cabernet
and watch me stretch
catlike before
devouring
this parchment

I will
dip my quill
tap off
the excess
navigate
whetted tip
toward
prostrate
virgin
sheet
and

press
down

let your
finger
trace
the fold
right here
where these
pages meet

scan the text
carefully
and
welcome
what you
discover
between
the
lines

save this place
because you will
want to come back
and re-read the pages

yet still
it is a

poor substitute
for skin

sleep bar

tiny box at my bedside
what power you possess
with one shrill burst
to launch me into day
with an addict's hunger

I am relishing these
last few crumbs of sleep
greedily captured beneath
my staggering fingertips

equestrian

rushing clipboard in hand
air thick with Betadine
I see the girl

no one has drawn
the privacy curtain, no time
as the ambulances roll in

she is 10 perhaps
mud-caked riding boots
on the floor below

a white tube protrudes
between pale lips
lifeless eyes staring upward

this morning, perhaps she had
nibbled a bagel, brushed her teeth
giggled about a boy

the earth on her pants is still damp
the smell of horse sweat still fresh

she is so … exposed
lying still amid this ruckus

so I slowly pull the curtain along its track
while outside the girl's parents park their car,
rush in to the clean wide counter

eager for news

nebula

hiding inside the nebula
this life seems like
a slow armageddon

a cardboard cut-out
of myself dangles from
a cheap wire hanger

three sharp blasts
constitute the extortion
of my acceptance

we are mining for ochre
or the telltale lipstick stains
our fossils of understanding

woman or satellite dish
overwhelmed with what
has been harvested

repositioning the antennae
left, right, ... down
into the nether regions

feel the pull of wanting
all the while crouching
naked inside the nebula

4:30 a.m., interstate 26 heading west

windows down, the steering wheel solid in hand
invisible fingers begin to lift my untethered hair

I hush the console and listen while the damp July
whispers a heartfelt solace across the night

> *it is summer in South Carolina*
> *and I am obsessively sad*

pavement rolls out gray before my headlights perforated
white lines blinking past like an old movie projector

lonely is a spirit with four lanes of tarmac to ponder
existential bedtime stories of how things might have been

ahead, a rolling tomb of steel and mesh dynamic
crosses into view – 1,000 souls heading to the slaughter

vestiges of their genetic code, picked up by the ether,
dance across my windshield like massive snowflakes

> *it is summer in South Carolina*
> *and I am obsessively sad*

brutal assigns present these souls their last sensory scraps
hot diesel wind and the random popping of firecrackers

they won't feel the blade, just the sudden blow, the jarring
of nerve endings, and the final plunk of weight to conveyor

Soul Mate No. 760

he said he was
'a little bit militant'

go ahead, apply
your metaphors

this brewing storm
a restless sea
the pacing lion

he is an arrogant nomad
a bridge to nowhere

intense and aloof
bitter and occasionally sweet

raised index finger
has to take this call
turns his back to me

well hello there
Soul Mate No. 760
I recognize you now

peeling

the dark blue polish on her
blunted fingernails is peeling
her cuticles paint-stained

she grasps a charcoal pencil
and slowly commences a
gentle tracing of the phallus

pausing, she reaches
for the mimosa in a highball glass
drinks while considering

like the lover whose needfulness
quickly ended her desire
this will exist in the abstract

another sip of cool sweet yellow
a glance out at the street
she saves the color for last

Anastasia

Sinatra boots, girlish curves, chiffon
Amber locks in gossamer movement
She whispers a Cheshire invitation
As wildflowers lean in her direction

Art Bar Ramblings II

Deafening fragrance of clove and leather blend patchouli and rouge over sidemeat. Everywhere karma improvises decadence and intellect. Motorcyclers, wrestling fans, comic book heroes, blue-collar lovers, nerds, rappers, poets, and queers mingle, bitch, flirt, and compare tattoos. Give me a marker for the can. Three a.m. leave-behind philosophy – immortality purchased with ink and saliva.

Sink your haunches into this plush beer-stained sofa and ask me if I care. Fuck my day job; I want to create art. Adore me, respect me, make love to me. Let's debate all these inequities but understand that, down the street, an undertaker burns the midnight oil. Whatever you do, be hip in death. The happy face people think this is a gay bar. What are we all if not gay, with a little help. Mix me something red with sweet Chambord and split it four ways. It's important to share the wealth.

Myrellen's Coat

They let her have a single needle.

She scavenged the rest
from box tops and laundry scraps.
It was her one dispensation.

> "She sews without purpose,"
> the ward notes proclaim,
> "is non-productive."

A red-maned waif on hands and knees,
ill-fitting hospital gown gathered about her,
scoured the icy tile floors for wanton fibers.

The staff described her as savage, uncontained.
Long shards of red hair seemed to clang
like wind chimes down her willowy back.

They were careful to avoid the swinging tresses
for fear of being cut, but she tried to explain
that it really didn't hurt after awhile.

She stitched feverishly, day and night,
addresses, birthdays, children's rhymes,
meandering colors across the white cloth.

> "She sews without purpose,"
> the ward notes proclaim,
> "is non-productive."

The needle is her deliverance.
Pierce, penetrate, and pull through,
feel the drag, the curt resistance.

In painstaking detail,
the thread marries fabric
to tell her tale of abandon.

Embroidered vowels and lamentations
form a scarf, a dress, a waistcoat –
her frantic wardrobe of release.

failure

what we have here
is a failure

all the while he thinks
I'm not into him
and I think
he's not into me

and so we continue
this long dance of wanting

a flash of his thigh
peeks out of the blanket
as he turns in sleep
on my regretful sofa

this wakening
so stunning
so palpable

torture

I want I want I want

indeed

what we have here
is a failure

lotus revisited

spirits of evening past
cradle their bodies
against faded linen
softened by tender leavings

within the earliest glow
rouse cursory thoughts
of Phuket mushrooms
and crisp spring rolls

warm-skinned scent
of lovers sleeping
stomach to back
in reflexive embrace

the voyeur of day
most enchanting dawn
captures their still profiles
in perfect visual cadence

she is first to stir
drawn to breathe in
his familiar energy
rapt with carnal prospect

leg casual over thigh
with cunning pressure applied
to pull him agreeably away
from his ingenuous slumber

first kiss brings moisture
to dry lips and the
mildly sour signature
of a long night's fast

dual pulses engage
the subtle promptings
of tongues and fingers
to known pleasure points

their eyes touch knowing
as a Napa vintner slowly
uncorks a dusty bottle
so this ripe new day

can breathe

peppermint

his mouth
on mine
lips parted
he breathes

peppermint

and it is true

a cool repast
before we begin again
fingertip appetizers
slick wet decadence
the candle leaves
a suggestion
shaped by the ink
on his russet skin
moving above me
our knowing cocoon
lover's cadence
downy whispers
an urgent pulse
this one-ness
completed
by a sigh
of penetration

gush of scent

our hot
sweet
protected
embrace

haiku 3

little red Buddha
you remind me to prosper
my sweet workplace friend

sparrow

gently she lay her head on the twigs
to stare into the eyes of the dying sparrow
its chest moved rapidly up and down
otherwise the bird was quite still
a large drop of rain struck its wing, making a small splatter
and she began to hear big fat drops falling about them
striking the leaves and ground sporadically
how fragile yet stalwart this little being was
soon its breathing became slower
and she felt a subtle shift in energy
then the bird tucked its wings
and let the brown stillness swaddle it
while she gazed into its fading eyes
the bird regarded her with acceptance
how curious to watch
this creature embrace its fate
she knew the instant it changed
became an empty vessel
and there was absolute loveliness
in its passing

nesting instincts

through the enduring migrations
it is essential to feather your nest
with fine art and literature

worms will go only so far
like take-out chinese vegetables
that only leave you wanting

open wide your mind and let words
slide down your throat
savor notes that linger in the sinuses

learn to write and think deliberately
because we all understand
the mother doesn't always return

this is when darwin's pen makes clear
why some can fly without being taught
and others fall to the ground, are still

feather your nest with fine art and literature
then jump from the tree; let the colors
and language carry you to new heights

ABOUT THE AUTHOR

Kristine Hartvigsen is a freelance writer based in Columbia, South Carolina. She serves as associate editor of *Jasper* Magazine: The Word on Columbia Arts. She also is a past editor of *South Carolina Business* and *Lake Murray-Columbia* magazines as well as a past contributing editor of *undefined* magazine.

A self-taught poet and photographer with a degree in education from the University of South Carolina, she was a finalist in the South Carolina Poetry Initiative's Single Poem Contest in 2010 and 2011. The eclectic and mostly unrelated mix of poems in this collection represent Hartvigsen's explorations of different styles and forms over many years.

ABOUT MUDDY FORD PRESS

Muddy Ford Press is a family-owned publishing company located in Chapin, South Carolina and dedicated to providing boutique publishing opportunities for South Carolina writers and poets.

Contact us at MuddyFordPress.com.

www.ingramcontent.com/pod-product-compliance
Lightning Source LLC
Chambersburg PA
CBHW032017290426
44109CB00013B/688